If I Could Speak

Letters from the Womb

Scripture quotations are from *The Holy Bible, English Standard Version*, copyright © 2001 by Crossway Bibles, a publishing ministry of Good News Publishers. Used by permission. All rights reserved. ESV Text Edition: 2011.

Copyright © Mark Jones 2019

ISBN 978-1-5271-0466-2

First published in 2019

by

Christian Focus Publications Ltd,
Geanies House, Fearn, Ross-shire,
IV20 1TW, Scotland
www.christianfocus.com

A CIP catalogue record for this book is available from the British Library.

Printed in Ukraine.

Creative design by Jorge R. Canedo E.
Photography by Emmy Lou Virginia Canedo E.
Illustrations by Grace Pederson

If I Could Speak

Letters from the Womb

Introduction

This book is written from a particular angle that requires some indulgence from the reader. All people find themselves in a unique situation, especially expecting mothers. We all have a story to tell; we all have various explanations for our actions; and we all aim, to some extent, to excuse ourselves for the choices we make that perhaps cause us a crisis of conscience.

This short book takes a fictional scenario of a preborn child, roughly twenty weeks old, who writes letters to her mother. She puts forth a case for why her mother should decide to keep her and raise her instead of having an abortion. Hence the title, *If I Could Speak: Letters From the Womb*. Naturally, if one of us were in a life or death situation and we could write letters to the person who had the authority and ability to grant us life or end our life, we would give an impassioned case. I trust readers will understand that perspective and even aim to empathize with the child.

While this book is for everyone, it is specifically aimed to give expecting mothers who are considering an abortion, something to think about before they decide to make a choice to end another person's life. I applaud such people reading this book for even entertaining a different perspective that may cause them some discomfort and even change their mind. Thank you for reading.

There are many on both sides of the debate that are so convinced that no amount of writing will likely change their minds on the issue. But there are some who genuinely struggle with the reality of having an abortion. This book aims especially to convince those mothers and fathers who are still undecided on this hugely important topic.

The pictures are also designed to move the reader. I make no apologies for including them. Words and visible pictures are powerful tools when used properly. I trust that a fair-minded reading of this book will give you, the reader, much to think about.

Dear Mommy,
I can hear your voice.

Dear Mommy,

I can hear your voice.

You're probably surprised to receive this letter from me. I'm the person living inside of you, your fetus ('offspring'). I'm your child.

I'm a girl (sorry to ruin the surprise), but I don't believe I have a name yet. I've heard that others receive their names quite early: some as soon as their mom is aware there is a child inside and they can determine whether the child is a boy or girl. But others are named when they are delivered from the womb, such as my cousin, Darren, who aunt Delores thought was going to be a girl because of her 'woman's intuition.' And some, I've heard, but cannot believe, never get a name at all. I'm happy to trust you with a good name, but please don't call me Betsy, Barb, or Bernace.

There's a lot I want to talk to you about. I am your child, after all, and we generally like to talk! These letters are my way of speaking to you.

I think you should know a little about how I'm doing physically. Please be patient: what I'm about to tell you is rather complex stuff, but my letters after this one will be less scientific.

As you know, everything started out well; my dad's sperm fertilized your oocyte and formed a zygote. This fertilization (conception) produced me, also known as a diploid cell or primordium. My life from conception has been a continuous process, but fertilization was the critical point because that's when I, a new genetically distinct person, was formed. I existed from conception as a genetic unity when the combination of 23 chromosomes from each parent resulted in the 46 chromosomes in the zygote. I'd like to thank you both for providing me with the chromosomes needed for life. Please pass on my thanks to my dad.

My development has been nothing short of amazing. At around three weeks since your last menstrual cycle the sperm broke through the tough outer membrane of your egg and fertilized it. Days later the fertilized zygote (me) arrived in your uterus. I was a tiny ball (a blastocyst).

At about four weeks I was the size of a poppy seed. Like teenagers, I entered a pretty rough stage in my appearance at five weeks where I looked sort of like a tadpole, but your belly protected me from anyone making fun of my looks. My heart began to beat this week, which is amazing considering I'm about the size of a sesame seed. At six weeks, my nose, mouth, and ears took shape. I wonder whether I'll have a Greek or Roman or Aquiline nose or a bulbous tipped nose like you. My intestines and brain developed too, although my brain still has a long way to go and I'm really hoping I am not sensitive to gluten like you, mom.

Seven weeks was a major stepping-stone for me: my feet and hands emerged from my developing arms and legs, but I still had that unseemly tail. You were not aware of this, but at eight weeks I started moving due to my developing lungs. At this point I was about the size of a kidney bean. By nine weeks that embryonic tail thankfully disappeared, and this is when I started to gain weight quickly.

Around ten weeks signaled the completion of my most critical phase of development and, well, I'm happy to report that I'm looking a lot better these days than I was in those awkward weeks before. In fact, even my nails formed – a free pedicure of sorts! Eleven weeks was when I was almost fully formed. I basically do hot yoga most of the day inside of you, with kicking, stretching, and some hiccupping due to my developing diaphragm. But you didn't feel a whole lot at that point. If you're curious, I was about the size of a fig at eleven weeks – oh, and don't tell Grandma, but I think I'm left-handed.

At twelve weeks I was basically the Karate Kid. My reflexes kicked in and my fingers opened and closed: 'Wax on, wax off!' In the final week of your first trimester, my fingerprints were detectable and my skin showed my organs and veins. Can you believe that my ovaries contained more than two million eggs at this point?

Getting past the first trimester was a huge step for us: miscarriages usually happen in the first trimester, but are far less likely after that. I don't want to sound too confident, but I'm in a physically safer zone (for now). I hope you're feeling better now from your morning sickness and able to get back to your regular exercise routine. Remember, interval training is better than a constant jog. Test the limits of your heart (pun intended).

After my fifteenth week I could sense light; and entering my sixteenth week is perhaps when you might have felt me kick. Remember that avocado you had for lunch? Well, I was almost that size. Seventeen weeks was pretty cool for me. Besides my joints moving more freely, my skeleton, which was formerly soft cartilage, started to harden to bone. I went through a sporty phase at eighteen weeks. Like boys in high school, I did a lot of flexing and you may have felt these movements. And now I am nineteen weeks, 6.0 inches long and weighing in at about 8.5 ounces, the size of a peach.

My senses are all developing and one of my favorite things is happening now: I can hear your voice. Can you please keep talking to your friends and singing in the shower? And, wow, I really love it when you laugh; it's like a mini–earthquake in here when you do!

I can hear your voice.

Love,
...

I can hear your voice.

Love,

...

Dear Mommy,
I would make you happy.

2

Dear Mommy,

I would make you happy.

People speak a lot about the pursuit of happiness. I sometimes wonder if you are happy. Are you?

People also speak a lot about depression. It can feel like a state of (extreme) dejection, whereby the depressed have a mood of hopelessness and feelings of inadequacy. Most depressed people feel as though there's a downward pressure upon them, though it is very often hard to put into words. This 'pressure' drains their energy for life, with simple tasks becoming like hikes up a mountain. Paralyzed in their mind and body, there is often a lack of desire, drive, and decisiveness. Constant negativity replaces joyful expectations of what the day may bring. The ability to respond sanely to trials, setbacks, and criticism is thwarted either by total indifference or outbursts of anger that causes greater melancholy than before.

In one sense, depression and unhappiness don't make sense to me. The world has so much to offer. What an exciting place with rivers, mountains, and trails. Cities, towns, and villages – all featuring variations of architecture and human brilliance – adorn this earth. The refreshing rain and the warmth of the sun provide sensations on our bodies as we walk, run, bike, or – ahem! – push strollers. There are a variety of foods and drinks, which I'm told extend beyond breast-milk! The music I hear from time to time also sounds delightful and occasionally soothing, though I don't particularly enjoy certain music on the radio as you drive singing along (often getting the words wrong; FYI, in the one song it is 'I just need one more shot at forgiveness' not 'I just need one more shot, half a Guinness').

So how is it that people are unhappy? What is going wrong out there?

Some people are depressed or unhappy through no fault of their own. Trauma or abuse can cause depression, just as the loss of a loved one can. Others, however, are unhappy because in their pursuit of happiness they have abused the good. Whether sex or alcohol, friends or money, work or play, we have an uncanny ability to take good things and make them bad because they exercise a far greater influence than they were designed to offer. We pursue happiness at all costs, even if it costs us our happiness.

The more people pursue pleasure for the sake of pleasing themselves the unhappier they seem to become. As a result, many – especially the wealthy – are depressed because of their greed. Instead of out-going love towards others, including patience, kindness, and gentleness, the extreme love of self has not helped but hindered those seeking happiness. If it really is more blessed (happy) to give than receive, why do people snatch and grab so much?

I know, mom, you're going to give me a lot of advice over the course of my childhood and probably as long as we're both alive. I know I'm going to sometimes ignore or reject your advice. Sorry. It must be difficult to know what is right for someone but have that person reject what is good.

If you are unhappy now, or have been unhappy in the past (and you remember the horrible feelings associated with such a state), I want to assure you that I will try my best to contribute to your overall happiness. My first smile, word, steps, recital, and soccer goal will be joyful moments. The first card I make for your birthday or the first mother's day art project you receive will, I promise, not make you sad. My smile on the swing as you push me will provoke in you a smile, just as my A in physical education on my report card will cause you to beam with pride over my (our?) athletic prowess. I can't promise much on Math given your own history, but I'll do my best. When you tell me not to eat lollipops before breakfast I'll only lick them instead.

You know what else may make you happy? Knowing that all of the hard work you invest in me, from conception, to birth, to graduation, will give you great satisfaction and joy. Hard work deserves reward. I want to reward you in different ways for the hard work you will invest in me. I would like the chance, mommy.

So many 'things' in this world promise happiness: phones, computers, money, success, early retirement, etc. But how many of these always deliver on what they promise? 'Real happiness is cheap enough, yet how dearly we pay for its counterfeit' (Hosea Ballou).

I can tell you what always delivers on what is promised: mutual love. Quite apart from all of these special moments mentioned above, you need to know that even when I'm not giving you a card or baking you a cake or bringing you a sweater to put on when you're cold, I will always have a disposition of love towards you. After all, you are my mom; and as natural as it is for me to breathe, it should be as natural for us to love each another.

People do crazy things when they are not loved. But love makes difficult situations worth it. Love gives happiness a strong foundation.

All of this is to say, I hope to be a constant source of love and happiness in your life. I won't be perfect; I won't always listen; I shall have my own dark days; and I may give you tears of sadness from time to time. But, ultimately, I'm rather confident and hopeful that your invested love in me will do wonders not only for me but also for you (and others). It is better to give than receive, I'm told. Happy people are giving people. Giving people are loving people.

I would make you happy.

Love,
....

I would make you happy.

Love,

....

Dear Mommy,
You and daddy put me here.

3

Dear Mommy,

You and daddy put me here.

One of the wonderful things about being a human is our ability to make rational free decisions, especially those decisions for the good of others. But one of the scary things about being a human is the undeniable fact that our decisions have consequences, which can affect others either positively or negatively. Think of Hitler's decisions and the consequences for millions of innocents. Or, positively, think of Denis Mukwege. He was the winner of the 2018 Nobel Peace Prize. As a gynecologist he spent over twenty years treating (over 46,000) injured women in the Democratic Republic of Congo. Here's his testimony, which is deeply moving:

'Most of the time, it's easier to close eyes, close ears, and say, It's not my problem. I don't have expertise. I can't do anything. Then, you have your peace. But I think this is a bad way. When people decide to be indifferent, the consequences are terrible. I say to everyone, "You can do something." Everyone can learn. Everyone can be there for each other. And it doesn't have to be big. Just compassion can change someone's life, showing them empathy. Just to approach someone with your heart and share the humanity of another. That can change the world.'

How can we not aim to share in this attitude towards our fellow human beings? Strange how the world celebrates a man who has this attitude towards those outside of the womb; but if he saved as many in the womb I wonder if he would receive a Nobel Prize?

This brings me to my main reason for writing you this letter: we can either choose to live in a society where we are prepared to account for our decisions or we can pretend that we don't really need to be responsible for our actions. The former requires a great deal of self- sacrifice whereas the latter requires selfishness, with the latter apparently coming a lot easier to us than the former.

Based on the conversations I hear from time to time, Nick asks you about me. I take it you are the ones both responsible for my existence. He must be my dad. I'll write to him later.

But if I understand the process of creating a baby, is it fair to say that you and Nick enjoyed consensual sexual intercourse and did not prevent conception from taking place with the full awareness of the possible consequences (or blessing)? As Mark Twain said, 'Familiarity breeds contempt — and children.' Your right to choose what to do with your body meant that you, by virtue of your actions, chose me. I think that's the logical implication of your rational, free actions with Nick.

Sadly, I hear that some women were literally forced to have sex against their will, but I'm thankful to hear that you and my dad had (have?) affection for each other when I came into existence.

Now, I'm not a rocket scientist, but I don't believe that I forced myself upon either of you. Even those children conceived in a tragic situation (i.e., rape), did not force themselves upon anyone. So here I am, I can do no other. Through no decision of my own, living inside of you, I constantly wonder what will happen to me. I've sensed in your talk that you're quite troubled by the fact of my existence in your belly.

I want to ask you very seriously: Am I an unwanted guest who arrived because of decisions you and my dad made? I don't want to make you feel too guilty, but I do want to know why two rational, consenting adults can make a decision (for immediate enjoyment purposes) but also question whether they should be accountable for the possible effects of their actions.

As Ann B. Ross once said, 'I certainly supported a woman's right to choose, but to my mind the time to choose was before, not after the fact.'

I know you intuitively expect that others in this world, and especially in your immediate circle of relationships, should be accountable for their actions. Remember when you were so irate at that drunk driver who took the life of that innocent child who was coming home from her basketball practice? You called for justice, claiming that the driver should be held responsible for his decision to drink too much and then get behind a wheel. Every day we live with these expectations. It would be impossible to live and function without a strong sense that actions have consequences and also that certain responsibilities follow our actions.

Do you not think it reasonable for me to simply ask you and daddy whether you are both prepared to be responsible for putting me here in your belly?

You and daddy put me here.

Love,
....

You and daddy put me here.

Love,

...

Dear Mommy,
I would like a name.

Dear Mommy,

I would like a name.

I've really been enjoying your Jim Croce music, which I first heard when you were watching a *Stranger Things* episode. Call me old fashioned, but I actually like songs with meaningful lyrics. Croce's song, 'I've got a name,' got me thinking about my own possible name. Incidentally, this was the last song he sang before his ill-timed death in a plane crash. These were the words that have stayed with me:

> *'Like the pine trees lining the winding road*
> *I got a name, I got a name*
> *Like the singing bird and the croaking toad*
> *I got a name, I got a name.'*

I wish I could sing that song with you. But, alas, I don't have a name. I'm a girl. So while I've asked not to be named Betsy, Barb, or Bernace, maybe we can agree on a name?

I'd like to offer a suggestion: can you name me Zoe? I like that name; it doesn't need to be shortened; it has the 'ee' at the end, which sounds really cute when calling young children by their name. I'm sure you know what the name means, given your own Greek heritage: 'Life'!

Names are powerful identity markers of an individual. In the past, a name was chosen rather carefully because of what the name meant. Today, I think, people tend to choose names that sound nice rather than enquiring deeply into the meaning of the name.

When you hear the word 'Hitler' you think of the person who was responsible for the dehumanization of millions of Jews in Nazi Germany. He had a name, but many of those who suffered under his rule were essentially nameless.

From 1954 Yad Vashem ('A Memorial and a Name') has tried to recover the names of the millions of victims who died during the Holocaust. They have identified roughly 4.7 million so far. Every name is important; it represents a small undoing of the massacre that treated fellow humans as less than humans. For the Jewish people today, the recovery of a name from that period is one way to see the person as a person and not just a number.

In Eastern Europe where there were Nazi-occupied areas, it has been more difficult to recover names than from Western and Central Europe. During the Holocaust, roughly 1.5 million children were murdered, but only half have been identified. There are reports of parents who are named, but their children are unnamed. Because they were children, survivors were unable to remember their particular identities. Many have worked tirelessly to keep these children from being simply a statistic; they need to be remembered as humans with names.

Here is a letter from a seven-year-old Jewish boy called Edward-Edik Tonkonogi, which he wrote to his parents in 1941,

> *'Dear Mummy and Daddy,*
> *Today it has been raining all day.*
> *I am playing with Vitya and Grisha.*
> *I kiss and hug both of you very tight,*
> *Yours,*
> *Edik.'*

Sadly, the Nazis murdered Edik that same year. He is an example of the powerless at the mercy of the powerful. But at least we have Edik's name memorialized for us. That's something, isn't it?

I know this has been a sad letter. I'm sorry for that, but I just want you to know that whatever decision you make regarding my life, I'd like the honor and dignity of having a name. I don't want to be a nameless statistic, but wish to be remembered as a person. I think giving me a name honors that request.

I would like a name.

Love,
Zoe(?)

I would like a name.

Love,
Zoe(?)

Dear Mommy,
You were here once.

Dear Mommy,

You were here once.

Did you enjoy your surprise birthday party last night? Must have been a good time given the noise. You kept me up for ages, especially when Grandma got a hold of the karaoke machine despite vigorous protests from Grandpa. Congratulations on turning twenty-five, a quarter of the way till you get a letter from the Queen, right? Oh wait! This is the United States of America. Maybe the IRS will send you a letter?

So twenty-five years ago you made your grand entrance into this world. Grandma's story last night about your birth was hilarious. Grandma said she wouldn't budge from the toilet because she felt a bowel movement approaching. The nurse tried to get Grandma back to the delivery table so you wouldn't end up in the toilet. As Grandma moved toward the delivery table she had to push, and, in a squatting position, pushed you out with the doctor lying on her back like an auto mechanic. Grandma said you've been a lot easier to deal with since your birth, except for the time when she tried to teach you to drive.

But Grandma also gave some details about how you were a total surprise to both her and Grandpa. You were conceived when Grandpa was trying to make his way through College in order to become an accountant. Grandma was almost finished her nursing course, and, I guess, you just weren't the most convenient surprise. But Grandma and Grandpa were natural fighters, and figured they would make it all work somehow (which they did!). Grandma says she became a better nurse because of her pregnancy; she was better able to relate to other women who were having various emotional and physical difficulties during their pregnancies.

Whatever common discomforts women experience during pregnancy, Grandma seemed to embrace them all. Tiredness, morning sickness, headaches, backache, leg cramps, and some hair loss were the hallmarks of your time in Grandma's belly. But Grandma said she'd have suffered those things a thousand times over to experience the joy of seeing your face for the first time. You and Grandma clearly have a very close relationship. Okay, I know that you sometimes ignore her daily calls, but you're very sweet together.

You've had twenty-five pretty good years so far. But you've actually had twenty-five years and nine months. Like me, you spent time in a womb; you were cared for (fed), spoken of, rubbed, etc. Your mom, amidst so many uncertainties in her life, kept you at that time and also with many painful physical realities that come with pregnancy. I suppose from one angle, nothing could have been more inconvenient to Grandma at the time and yet her testimony last night displayed an attitude so very far from viewing you that way. When Grandma hugged you at the end of her speech, I could feel her, too. Three generations.

You were kept safely in her womb for nine months, growing and developing as I now am. You were brought into the arms of a loving person. Grandma wanted to name her child early on, even before she knew whether she was having a boy or a girl. So she settled on a name that could be suited to either a male or female. Hence your name: Alexis.

As you may know, Alexis means 'helper' or 'defender.' You are a helper and defender of persons. Just as you were once in Grandma's womb, now I am in precisely the same position you were. I am asking that you extend the same courtesy to me that was shown to you, Alexis.

You now enjoy basic safety and rights as a human being. Imagine you went to bed each night for the next several months knowing there is a person in this world that finds you to be a great inconvenience in their life. And imagine this person has carte blanche to come in and kill you at any time in the next several months without any ramifications. When you go to sleep you are helpless, so to speak, unaware of when or if you will make it through the night. You could say you were in such a position when you were in Grandma's womb. But you were kept safe because the person who carried you chose not to enter the 'house' and slay the helpless victim.

You were here once.

Love,
Zoe

You were here once.

Love,
Zoe

Dear Mommy,
I will take care of you one day.

6

Dear Mommy,

I will take care of you one day.

I've heard old age can be a challenging time, not just for the elderly, but also for those who deal with the elderly. Sweet little old ladies can get up to all sorts of trouble. Do you remember when great-grandma almost caused a riot on the golf course because she insisted on walking instead of driving the cart, which led to a massive pile-up of angry golfers waiting behind her group? Her friend Wang has pictures of most of it, until his friend Rodney told him to put the camera away since it was a golf course.

You're 25, but one day you'll be 75 and saying, 'Where did the time go?' With the addition of 50 years to your body you'll no doubt start to develop a whole host of issues, though people will stop making fun of you for being a hypochondriac.

Life goes on until we simply cannot go on. Usually, however, we don't just die without years of warnings that our bodies are slowly breaking down. I'm sorry to bring up your inevitable death, but, as you know, it is a reality I also deal with as well as every other person in this world. Taxes and death, mommy.

The amazing thing about old age is the way the elderly start to resemble little children, even babies. We could call it the circle of life. In a sense, if we live long enough, we return to the place we started in many ways. It is what scholars and writers have called a 'second childhood.' Whether frequent naps or the need for help walking or the need for diapers, there are many obvious similarities.

As William Shakespeare famously wrote in *As You Like It*:

> *'All the world's a stage,*
> *And all the men and women merely players;*
> *They have their exits and their entrances;*
> *And one man in his time plays many parts,*
> *His acts being seven ages. At first the infant,*
> *Mewling and puking in the nurse's arms;*
> *....*
> *And so he plays his part. The sixth age shifts*
> *Into the lean and slipper'd pantaloon,*
> *With spectacles on nose and pouch on side;*
> *His youthful hose, well sav'd, a world too wide*
> *For his shrunk shank; and his big manly voice,*
> *Turning again toward childish treble, pipes*

And whistles in his sound. Last scene of all,
That ends this strange eventful history,
Is second childishness and mere oblivion;
Sans teeth, sans eyes, sans taste, sans everything.'

It seems fair and right that the care you show towards me in my early years, whereby I'm especially dependent upon you for basic love and needs, should be reciprocated later in life when you will need me just as I needed you. I think a lot of children forget the sacrifices their parents made for them.

I've spoken to you a lot about your responsibilities towards me. But this letter is as much for me as it is for you. I need to make a promise that, if I am able, someone who not only loves you, but also owes a specific type of love towards you, will care for you.

Will I help you walk when you are unable? Will I feed you when you cannot feed yourself? Will I clean you and bathe you? Will I take you places and get you your medicine? Will I sing to you and tell you I love you? Will I put you to sleep or wake you up? Will I simply be there for you in the ways you will need me?

I hope so. Just as I ask to be honored as a person, I think you need to be honored as a person while you are alive. You have certain obligations towards me; but I will have certain obligations towards you. A loving relationship always entails mutual obligations.

Just as I hope you'll one day give me a bath and cleanse me, so I hope to return the favor. Just as I hope you'll continue to feed me, even channeling food into my mouth like an airplane landing, so I hope to feed you one day in the future food that will nourish your ailing body.

Perhaps consider your long-term future and ask, who will be there for you. Who do you want to take care of you when you need loving care?

I will take care of you one day.

Love,
Zoe

I will take care of you one day.

Love,
Zoe

Dear Daddy,
Happy Father's Day.

7

Dear Daddy,

Happy Father's Day.

While I'm alive it is always Father's Day, right? This letter that mom passed on to you isn't mistimed. You are a father.

You have successfully passed on your DNA so that there is now in this world a creature (me) who bears your resemblance in a myriad of ways. I am your offspring, just as you are the offspring of Grandma and Grandpa. By the way, do they know about me? I hear it is in my best interests to have grandparents, especially at birthdays and at Christmas.

How do you feel about me being 'daddy's little girl'? I am little, helpless, and ultimately fully dependent upon others right now for my existence. I am very needy. Sure, I'm doing my part in here, but I know I can't do this alone. If you can offer any help to mom and me, please do.

Many fathers, I am told, don't always want the child they are responsible for. They wanted and enjoyed the sex that brings about children, but for some reason they think it is okay to pursue pleasure but not responsibility. Sadly, such people generally live their lives that way...they love pleasure but avoid commitment and obligation. That's gutless, in my opinion.

A child wondrously emerges, yet we are merely viewed as a glob of cells without any real identity. Such a view helps many fathers avoid taking responsibility for their actions. They want to sleep easily at night, so they dodge investigating or thinking about what is really happening during sexual relations, knowing full well there is always the possibility that a new life is being created, even when 'protection' is used.

If I sound a little punchy, it is because I am. Maybe that's your DNA at work? Sorry...I guess. You see, I have one shot to convince you that I'm yours and worth keeping (not killing). In addition, you need to know that I am also worth investing in as a human being. I'm not so much after a reprieve from a death-sentence, though that would be nice. Rather, I'm asking you to make a commitment to raising me well and, I hope, being a good husband to mom. I need you both in my life; I need you both in love with each other in my life.

Whether mommy decides to keep me or not is in large part dependent upon whether you are willing to sacrifice for me while we are both alive. Many women suffer emotionally and psychologically for years (and years) after an abortion. They often suffer alone. I want to warn you that if you are unwilling to invest in me as a person for the rest of your life – even if I am ultimately born – then you may suffer emotionally and psychologically for many years, even the rest of your life.

Just listen to Eminem's song, 'River' (clean version), or 'Brick' by Ben Folds, and you'll understand what I mean. Flipsyde (ft. Piper), 'Happy Birthday' is powerful, too:

'Please accept my apologies, I wonder what would have been.
Would you have been a little angel or an angel of sin?
Tom-boy running around, hanging with all the guys.
Or a little tough boy with beautiful brown eyes.
I paid for the murder before they determined the sex,
Choosing our life over your life meant your death.
And you never got a chance to even open your eyes,
Sometimes I wonder as a fetus if you fought for your life.
Would you have been a little genius? In love with math?
Would you have played in your school clothes and made me mad?
Would you have been a little rapper like your poppa The Piper?
Would you have made me quit smoking by finding one of my lighters?
I wonder about your skin tone and shape of your nose,
And the way you would've laughed and talked fast or slow.
I think about it every year, so I picked up a pen.
Happy birthday, I love you whoever you would've been.'

I hope you don't ever have to read those words as one in the same position.

Did you know about Sinead O'Connor and her 1990 track called, 'My Special Child,' which highlights her grief over her abortion. In an interview, she was asked, 'What made you want to get an abortion?'

She answered: 'Well, I didn't really want to. The pregnancy had been planned, and I was madly in love with the father of the child. However, things didn't really work out between us. We were fighting. I was on tour, and I was feeling sick all the time. I didn't know what to do, and he wasn't really interested in the child. So I was left with the decision of whether or not to have the child, knowing that the father wasn't going to be around. I decided that it was better not to and that I would have a child at a later stage when his father would be around and involved. I didn't feel that I could handle it by myself.'

Do you see how important your role is in mom's decision?

The truth is, selfish people usually suffer emotionally and psychologically because they are never satisfied with the monster (themselves) that they need to feed. Such are monsters, that the more they are fed the less they are satisfied. Conversely, some of the happiest people are those who give, and give, and give. They find true joy because they don't need to fight against the air. The best way to receive is to give.

I want you to be happy, dad. Don't you want to be happy?

Your investment in my life and mom's will hopefully give you what you really desire. From what I've heard, a man has a natural desire to feel respected and honored for his hard work. Being a good husband and father is indeed hard work. But it is the type of work where the rewards usually outweigh the effort put in.

Can you really put a price on teaching me to ride a bike? Can you put a price on a picture I draw for you that lists my ten favorite things about dad? Can you put a price on my volunteer work for needy children, which happened because you led by example yourself? Can you put a price on the father-daughter dance we'll have at my wedding? If I may, can I suggest 'Unforgettable' by Nat King Cole,

'Unforgettable
In every way
And forever more
That's how you'll stay.'

Yes, daddy, 'Unforgettable' is how I'll stay.

Many things in life we can put a price on, such as monthly car payments for a Jag that breaks down too much or a slightly (massively?) over-priced Starbucks beverage. But there are some things money can't buy and those are the things in life that will give you true joy.

Why would you sacrifice so much possible joy? Your willingness to be a great dad will go a long way to both my survival and my welfare as a person in this world. You have the chance to influence so many lives by simply investing in one. Think about it, dad. Don't ignore the implications of your actions. Think about me. Think about us. Think about your grandchildren. Think about everything that is possible if you'll simply be a loving, responsible human being.

Your attitude in all of this is key. You can either try to convince mommy what is the right thing to do or you can, like so many others, pressure her to get rid of a 'problem.' There would be millions less children in my uncertain situation if their father's were willing to be just that: fathers.

Happy Father's Day.

Love,
Zoe

Happy Father's Day.

Love,
Zoe

Dear Mommy,
Your freedom and mine cannot be separated.

8

Dear Mommy,

Your freedom and mine cannot be separated.

In the mid-1980s Nelson Mandela was offered a conditional release from prison, but the terms of his release meant he was not going to be as free as a white South African. People, because of their race or, in my case, 'location' and size, have lacked certain fundamental rights over the course of world history.

In a statement read on his behalf by his daughter, Mandela asked:

'What freedom am I being offered when I must ask for permission to live in an urban area? What freedom am I being offered when I need a stamp in my pass to seek work? What freedom am I being offered when my very South African citizenship is not respected?'

It seems strange to me that many should publicly decry the system of apartheid in South Africa because non-whites lacked certain rights that whites enjoyed, but many of these same people feel that preborn children should not have any rights, such as the right to life, liberty, and the pursuit of happiness.

What rights do I have? Or, if I may ask you directly, what rights do you think I should have as a person? We are both human beings, but only the bigger, more developed person has rights. The smaller, more helpless person, does not have rights.

Interestingly, the Declaration on the Rights of the Child (1959) says,

'Whereas the child, by reason of [their] physical and mental immaturity, needs special safeguards and care, including appropriate legal protection, before as well as after birth,'

'Whereas the need for such special safeguards has been stated in the Geneva Declaration of the Rights of the Child of 1924, and recognized in the Universal Declaration of Human Rights and in the statutes of specialized agencies and international organizations concerned with the welfare of children,'

'Whereas mankind owes to the child the best it has to give.'

Mankind owes to the child the best it has to give by plucking preborn children from the womb, sometimes limb by limb?

There have been many atrocities over the course of world history whereupon certain classes of people have been subjugated because they were powerless. Do you not see how the preborn are the largest class of people in history to have suffered for no other reason than that they simply cannot fight back against the decision of their mother to abort them?

I believe that your rights and freedoms should not come at the expense of my rights to freedom and life. Mommy, I value your right to life, liberty, and the pursuit of happiness, but not at the expense of my own rights to those things, which we should both equally share.

As Nelson Mandela famously said at the end of his statement:

'Your freedom and mine cannot be separated.'

Love,
Zoe

'Your freedom and mine cannot be separated.'

Love,

Zoe

Dear Mommy,
God was here once.

9

Dear Mommy,

God was here once.

The Christian religion makes many sensational claims that, at first, seem quite ridiculous. But, when you take time to think about what is claimed, it is rather compelling.

We might argue, as many do, that the suffering and evil in this world is a reason not to believe in God. And yet the Christian religion claims that, far from being a casual observer of this mess, the eternal Son of God condescended and assumed to Himself a true human nature, consisting of both a body and soul. God the Son became a man and suffered, even to the point of death on a cross.

At the center of the Christian faith is the belief in the incarnation – the 'enfleshment' of the Son of God. In need of nothing because He possesses everything, the Son takes on a human nature (body & soul) so that He needs care from His mother from the moment of His miraculous conception.

When you think about it, it really is a beautiful story of God's love for humanity. What is the most precious thing in the universe to God the Father? For all of the value God places on each human being, who is made in His image, there is one person who occupies God's heart more than anyone else: Jesus Christ of Nazareth.

And where did God place the most precious person in the world?

In a womb.

The Almighty God, perfect in His being, and in need of nothing, sent His Son into the world to become a fetus that would be cared for by a virgin young lady. If anyone had a right to be terrified of what awaited her, consider Mary. Mary and Joseph did not have great financial means; they would find themselves fleeing to Egypt to protect their newborn boy; and one day Mary would see her Son publicly crucified at the hands of the Romans. But, from the beginning, she praised God for the gift He had given not just to her, but also to all mankind.

God did not send His Son to earth in the form of a grown man to live and die for our sins. Rather, God began with conception in the womb of the Virgin Mary. The safest place in the world for Jesus was His mother's womb. God so values the womb that He put his beloved Son there.

Perhaps we fail to grasp how incredible this truth is. God was placed in a womb. It is as shocking as the truth that God lay in a tomb. The Virgin Mary's womb was a designated safety zone where the Son of God's human nature would be formed with the utmost care.

God was not just showing the world how much He loves the world by offering His only begotten Son as a sacrifice for sinners; He was also showing the world that He values women and the safety zone known as the womb.

The Christian faith shows us that God loves the womb of a woman. He created the womb for His Son to dwell in at the most vulnerable stage of His earthly life. By extension, God has done the same for each of us. The womb is God's designated place of safety, but now it has become the most unsafe place in the world, with approximately 42,000,000 abortions taking place worldwide in 2018. That's like wiping out the population of Canada and then some each year, which is sad to think about because Canadians are just so nice.

I find it compelling that God shows His power to us in weakness. He becomes a baby, dependent upon His mother. I mean, think about it: if Jesus is both fully man and fully God then He was at once upholding this universe and yet was also being upheld in the womb of His mother. As He cried upon entering the world, He was entering our grief.

If you were going to make up a religion, then surely you wouldn't make up what the Christian faith claims. To say that God enters the world in a womb and later finds Himself in a tomb, only to be raised again from the dead, seems to be something only God could conceive.

In any case, I am comforted by the fact that not only are you reading this letter, but also God sees me. He knows me; He loves me. And I believe He wants me to have the privilege of living my life under His rule and for His glory.

Say what you want about the Christian faith, but we can't accuse the God of the Bible of not caring about the suffering and difficulties of the Christian life. Christ the Lord suffered, and the path to His life of suffering was through entering the world in a womb.

God was here once.

Love,
Zoe

Dear Mommy,
I'd rather be adopted than aborted.

Dear Mommy,

I'd rather be adopted than aborted.

Mommy, you know that I prefer to be with you and daddy. I want to see you grow old as you see me grow into adulthood. You're my first choice.

But, if you feel you are unable to raise me, given what you are saying out loud to others, I am asking that you will please consider giving me to someone who will be able to take care of me and give me a chance at life. By giving birth to me you are giving me a chance to have a valuable, fulfilling life. Not only that, someone else wants to be a parent and, for whatever reason, they are either unable or they want to add to their family via adoption. You will not only give me a shot at life, but you will enable someone to possibly achieve their dream of being a parent, even for the first time.

I can't help but think of those who will be blessed by this selfless action: me, my adoptive parents, and you will also feel good about your decision to grant me life rather than take my life. The possible regret and heartache you will feel if I am terminated will not exist if you choose to grant me this wish of growing up.

If you are curious, I think you can choose to have an open adoption so that you can see how I have done in life. I will try my best to make you proud that you did the right thing. I hope the smiles on my face, my successes and failures, will satisfy you enough that it was worth it to have me.

Perhaps you can consider that if I am aborted there is an obvious finality to it all. There's no going back once I am killed. If you decide to give me up for adoption, it may be possible that you'll change your mind and decide to keep me. Up until you sign the legal consent, you can decide to keep me. Personally, I'm hoping that if I'm delivered there will be an overwhelming sense of joy that will cause you to let me fall on your breasts and drink away with unmitigated joy, knowing I am sticking with you. Of course, this isn't always the experience of most breast-feeding mothers, but I think the joy and peace will come from knowing that you've done the right thing and that we can make this work.

I know thousands and thousands of women in America are getting pregnant at inconvenient times, sometimes even in the middle of their college education. And I know there is an apparently 'easy' option. Who wants to be seen 'with child' at College? But does convenience really take precedence over the life of another helpless human being?

Giving birth may be inconvenient to many. But that inconvenience is a small price to pay for the preservation of an innocent life, don't you think? Adoption means there is another choice you can make, since 'choice' seems to be omnipotent. If you must be pro-choice, then can I ask you to choose adoption?

Do you remember that man who fixed your roof the other day? He couldn't stop speaking about his kids. He was beaming with pride, knowing that the only thing of real consequence he's done for this world is provide humanity with three wonderful children, who have in turn given the world another six children. That was particularly moving, especially given all he had achieved, having attained an MBA despite an underprivileged upbringing and the loss of his father at a young age. That man was adopted. His mom carried him to full-term and granted to him an adoption into a family that did their best. I'm sure the man – Kevin, I think was his name – would happily say to you: I'm so thankful to my birth mom and my adoptive mom. I wouldn't be here without either of them. Two women in his life made him who he is and, I think, he harbors no resentment towards his mom for her decision to give him up for adoption.

I'd rather be adopted than aborted.

Love,
Zoe

I'd rather be adopted than aborted.

Love,

Zoe

Dear Mommy,
I wish I were a baby eagle.

11

Dear Mommy,

I wish I were a baby eagle.

I hope you never break an eagle egg intentionally and get caught.

Under the Bald and Golden Eagle Protection Act (1940) you can be fined a lot of money and even face time in prison if you destroy an eagle egg.

The eagle eggs are not left to themselves. Rather, the mother and also the father must keep the eggs warm. They need to protect the eggs from harsh sunlight, blistering cold, and also from predators (including human beings, I imagine). It truly is moving to see in the animal world the manner in which mothers protect their young, even laying down their lives, if necessary, for their preborn and born young.

Besides incubation, the eggs are turned once an hour so that they are evenly heated. As they are turned, the parents ball up their talons in order to prevent their claws from harming the eggs. It is amazing the care that goes into protecting the eggs from the parents. They will do anything, it seems, to ensure the survival of the egg.

Even in snow storms the parents must do whatever it takes to shelter their babies. There are videos of parents protecting their young in very harsh conditions. The parents can often huddle close together to provide extra warmth to protect the eggs and each other.

In one case, a mother incubated her chicks with the snow falling and didn't leave the nest almost the whole night. The next morning the male came to take over the incubating responsibilities, but minutes later the mom returned and took back her position as the chief caregiver for her young.

There's a natural instinct in the animal kingdom to protect the young and needy. We would think it very odd if we observed animals purposely eating poisonous food so as to murder their children. Scientists would be aghast and amazed at something so contrary to nature. We would even say a mutation has happened in the so-called 'evolutionary' process. I mean, as far as evolution is concerned, one of the main goals of animals is to leave offspring (DNA) behind in order that the stronger may survive. So to kill one's offspring is a fundamental reversal of the evolutionary process.

Baby bald eagles enjoy greater protection before birth than I do. They are no longer endangered (since 2007), but they are nonetheless protected, as they should be. But there is no such act for me. I remain, unlike the baby eagle, unprotected.

When society gives more rights to an eagle in an egg than a human in a woman by arguing that it is okay for a mother to kill her child yet acknowledging that a mother eagle would never kill her young, then we need to start asking serious questions about whether animals are more loving creatures than we are.

I wish I were a baby eagle.

Love,
Zoe

I wish I were a baby eagle.

Love,
Zoe

Dear Mommy,

I'm scared.

12

Dear Mommy,

I'm scared.

I'm almost twenty weeks now. This gives me some hope since most abortions are done before the twelfth week. But a second trimester abortion seems much scarier and crueler than a first trimester abortion, which leaves me petrified. I heard the doctor tell you it is called a Dilatation and Evacuation (D&E).

You should know that at twenty weeks I can feel pain in your womb, with even greater intensity than adults. You no doubt have felt me move by now, so you know I am there.

The D&E procedure is a surgical abortion whereby the abortionist will dilate your cervix and then insert instruments to dismember me and extract me from your uterus. I'll know if you plan to go through with this because the abortionist would use laminaria, which opens up your cervix 24-48 hours before the procedure.

From what the doctor said, the abortionist will insert a large suction catheter into your uterus in order to empty it of the amniotic fluid. When the fluid is removed, the sopher clamp (an instrument with sharp 'teeth') will pull my arms and legs from my body. After that, my intestines, spine, heart, lungs, and any other parts remaining will be torn out. I think I heard that the trickiest part of the abortion is finding, grasping, and crushing my head. Once my skull is removed, the abortionist will use a curette to clean out the uterus, remove the placenta, and thus any remaining parts of my body.

Like a child completing a puzzle, often the abortionist will put all my parts back together to make sure there are two arms, legs, and the rest of the body.

I want you to know that I will fight. As a helpless, dependent baby I don't stand much of a chance. But imagine I had the ability to really fight back and overcome the intruder and kill him/her. I wonder how they would feel? Do I have that right to protect myself by fighting back against my killer?

If you go to that clinic tomorrow I know that my fight will be short-lived, a testimony to my life here on earth. I know that I will not overcome the murderous intruder. After all, the abortionist has an unfair advantage: weapons of warfare. I've got my arms and legs to kick and punch, but that's about it.

I think I'm starting to understand how Helga Weiss felt. With her mother, she was sent to four Nazi concentration camps. She kept a diary, which we can read today. As she waited in a queue at Auschwitz she prayed she wouldn't die after her mother. The thought of being left alone was too harrowing. Remarkably, Helga is one of about 100 children who survived Auschwitz out of the roughly 15,000 who were sent there from the concentration camp at Terezín. At Terezín she survived in part because she was with her mother.

In Auschwitz (October, 1944) her diary records some remarkable occurrences. In one place Helga writes:

> 'They're taking mothers away from their children. I know that girl there; she's going to the right and her mum's going left. But the mum's quite old; she's got grey hair. My mum still looks young. But...maybe I look too much like a child? Maybe they'll ask me how old I am. Should I tell the truth? Fifteen; no, that's too little – they'd separate me from Mum. I'd better say I'm older, 18. Do I look it? Maybe they'll believe me.'

How beautiful to see these words of a young girl's desperate hope to be with her mom and not separated from her. I understand her words, profoundly. In another place, Helga describes the sights in Auschwitz:

> '...We're all starting to get nervous...it's a huge camp. I can see people, but what are they wearing? It looks like pyjamas, and they've all got the same ones.
>
> My God, those are prisoners' clothes! Where have they taken us?! This is a concentration camp! There are some men working over there, stacking boards.
>
> Why is that man beating them so hard? It must hurt horribly, he took a cudgel to them. How can he be so cruel?'

I understand, in part, Helga's sentiments. Against the odds, she survived. But most did not. She was nervous, and quite rightly. She heard, 'Ihr seid in Vernichtungslager!' ('You are in an extermination camp'). I guess I am in an extermination chamber as well. What shall my fate be?

This may be my last letter. Who knows? Only you and God.

I'm scared.

Love,
Zoe

I'm scared.

Love,
Zoe

Dear Mommy,
There is forgiveness.

Dear Mommy,

There is forgiveness.

Whether a child is 2 days old, 2 weeks old, 2 months old, or 2 years old, taking their life is murder. No one in my position will say anything different. If you were to gather all of the children in the world right now who are in a womb and allowed them to delegate together at an international conference, they would not need long to come back with a statement that abortion is murder. Let's face it, getting a few people to agree on anything today isn't easy, but I think we could get a unanimous opinion on this one among millions of delegates.

Moral relativism is a dangerous option. What's to stop a country enacting a law whereby parents are allowed to legally kill a child up to the age of five if they do not like how the child is working out for them? So far, our moral compass today does not allow such savagery, but in some countries, like Canada, there is no law protecting the preborn. A child can be minutes from entering the world and the mom can decide to end that child's life.

If we have a concept of right and wrong – an idea that believes that right and wrong are not mere cultural dictates – then what if we have done wrong?

Many people make a distinction between good and bad people. But, of course, we have to have an idea of who fits the good and who fits the bad? What are the criteria for such a division of persons? Where do we draw the line on a good person versus a bad person? It seems easy when you compare Hitler or Stalin to Mother Theresa, but most people's lives are more complex when evaluating their goodness/badness.

Just as science proves that human life begins from conception and thus there is no other objective way to determine when a fetus becomes a person, so there is no objective way to determine whether a person is good or bad apart from a Lawgiver making that judgment.

In the Bible we are told that all have sinned and fall short of the glory of God. I suppose it is one of the continually verifiable claims of the Bible, namely, human sinfulness. We are always arguing that others are wrong, crazy, evil, etc. We must have an objective standard in order to make such claims.

The bad news for us all is that none of us have lived a perfect life in which all of our thoughts, words, and actions have been perfectly pleasing to God or beneficial to our fellow humans.

God knows all and sees all; He sees the future better than we see the past few seconds. He heard you swear at that particularly slow driver the other day who didn't turn left fast enough at the advanced green light. He knew you would before you did. If He didn't, He would not be God.

There is good news about God: God the Father sent His Son into the world, via the womb, to live a life of absolute moral perfection. And not only that, but the sinless Son of God then died a gruesome death that He did not deserve in order to provide forgiveness for those who acknowledge they are bad and thus need forgiveness. He willingly laid down His life for the sake of His people He came to save.

The truth is, mommy, that you could decide to abort me, which would be sin, but if you later repented and asked for forgiveness from God He would gladly pardon your sins. He forgives all who ask. I'm not at all worried that saying this will give you a clear conscience if you decide to abort me. Because if you are moved by the truth that Christ laid down His life for sinners then you will certainly respond to such a truth in a way Paul says Christians should:

'For the love of Christ controls us, because we have concluded this: that one has died for all, therefore all have died; and he died for all, that those who live might no longer live for themselves but for him who for their sake died and was raised' (2 Corinthians 5:14-15).

If we believe and embrace Christ's death for our sins, then we will no longer live for ourselves but rather for Christ who showed the ultimate act of self-sacrificial love towards us. Such an attitude will then make the decision to keep me rather easy! His self-sacrifice for us, which cost Him His life, but gives us life everlasting, leads to our own small acts of self-sacrifice for others.

There is forgiveness now, freely offered, to all who acknowledge that they are living in a world where God is the one who not only determines what is right and wrong, but also provides a solution for those who have done wrong.

I hope such a message of love and forgiveness will grant you the peace that comes from trusting Jesus.

There is forgiveness.

Love,
Zoe

There is forgiveness.

Love,

Zoe

Dear Mommy,

I love you.

Dear Mommy,

I love you.

'How lucky I am to have something that makes saying goodbye so hard'
(A.A. Milne, Winnie-the-Pooh).

For me the beginning has turned out to be the end.

I love you; I wish you loved me too.

Zoe

Dear Zoe,

I miss you.

Dear Zoe,

I miss you.

It has been ten years since I chose to have an abortion.

A lot has happened in that time. Your dad and I married eight years ago. We are still childless, but we've tried in recent years without much success.

For the last several years I've worked with underprivileged children on a daily basis. Many of them do not have both parents in their home. But I try to bring some joy to their lives, even in small ways. There were many things you were right about concerning the joy that children can bring to one's life. I love their smiles when I bring my now 'world famous' brownies (without nuts, of course) for them to eat at snack time.

You should know there isn't a day that goes by without my remembering you. I see children laughing, crying, playing, singing, and I can't help but think what it would be like to see you do those things. I see moms and dads picking up their children from our after-school program and feel some sadness (and a bit of joy) when I see children running into the arms of their parents. And I heard Sinead O'Connor's song, 'My Special Child,' and it made me cry.

Your dad and I go out for dinner and as we see families I'm again reminded of what could have been. The kids' menu hasn't surfaced on our table yet with the coloring crayons. There are no colored pictures given to me.

One particularly bad moment occurred last week. I was going to the grocery store and a Girl Guide was selling her cookies. I didn't have cash, but I said, 'Oh, I love those cookies; I'm so sorry I can't buy one, but I don't have any money on me.' The girl, apparently moved by my love for her cookies, gave me a box and told me I didn't have to pay but I should pass on a kind deed to someone else. For some reason, I was reminded of your letters and thought that this Girl Guide is the girl I'm sure you could have been.

Now I am unable to have a child when I want a child. Before I was able but unwilling; now I'm willing but unable. Of late, Nick (dad) has been talking about adoption. And, again, I was reminded of your letter that you'd rather be adopted than aborted. I suppose adopting a child is one way of us honoring your request.

Anyway, I wanted to write this letter to you, knowing of course that you will never read it. But at least I'm able to say, given years of regret, that I'm sorry. Vain regrets aren't going to change what happened to you, but my 'sorry' comes from my heart. I'm not just sorry because I want a child now and can't have one. I'm sorry because I was given a gift and I refused to open it. I was wrong; you were right.

One last thing: it's Christmas time. Your dad and I are off to sing some carols and hymns at the Bible-believing church we both go to now. I'm looking forward to singing, 'Hark the Herald Angels Sing':

'Hark! The herald angels sing,
"Glory to the newborn King;
Peace on earth, and mercy mild,
God and sinners reconciled!"
Joyful, all ye nations rise,
Join the triumph of the skies;
With th'angelic host proclaim,
"Christ is born in Bethlehem!"'

Remember when you wrote, 'God was here once'? Indeed. And while there isn't a day that goes by that I don't think of you and what could have been, I am comforted by the fact that God has, through Jesus, forgiven me and given me peace (Psalm 103:12).

I miss you, but I am comforted by the hope that I may actually see you one day. That is my hope – a hope based on the gracious nature of God who gave His Son as a ransom for many, including Nick and me.

Love,
Mommy

I miss you.

Love,
Mommy

Christian Focus Publications

Our mission statement —

STAYING FAITHFUL
In dependence upon God we seek to impact the world
through literature faithful to His infallible Word, the Bible.
Our aim is to ensure that the Lord Jesus Christ is presented as
the only hope to obtain forgiveness of sin, live a useful life and
look forward to heaven with Him.

Our books are published in four imprints:

CHRISTIAN FOCUS

Popular works including biographies, commentaries, basic doctrine and Christian living.

CHRISTIAN HERITAGE

Books representing some of the best material from the rich heritage of the church.

MENTOR

Books written at a level suitable for Bible College and seminary students, pastors, and other serious readers. The imprint includes commentaries, doctrinal studies, examination of current issues and church history.

CF4•K

Children's books for quality Bible teaching and for all age groups: Sunday school curriculum, puzzle and activity books; personal and family devotional titles, biographies and inspirational stories — because you are never too young to know Jesus!

Christian Focus Publications Ltd,
Geanies House, Fearn, Ross-shire,
IV20 1TW, Scotland, United Kingdom.
www.christianfocus.com